Captivate Your Audience

Kirk House Publishers

Captivate Your Audience

Create Content that Connects Every Time You Present

Sara Krisher

Captivate your Audience Copyright © 2021 Sara Krisher

All rights reserved. This book or any portion thereof may not be reproduced or used in any manner whatsoever without the express written permission of the publisher except for the use of brief quotations in a book review.

Printed by Kirk House Publishers, in the United States of America.

First printing, August 2021

ISBN: 9781952976100
LOC: 2021902657

Cover Design: Ann Aubitz
Interior Design: Amy Davis

Kirk House Publishers
1250 East 115th Street
Burnsville, MN 55337
Kirkhousepublishers.com

This book is your
invitation to be authentic,
grow your confidence,
and share your thoughts and ideas.

TABLE OF CONTENTS

01	Foundation	Pg 13
02	Preparation	Pg 25
03	Creation	Pg 31
04	Connection	Pg 53
05	Reflection	Pg 69
06	Resources	Pg 74

Foreword

Congratulations! You are an expert on something, and you've been asked to present that expertise to some group of very intimidating folks. Your heart is racing, panic is creeping in, and you are watching your heart rate increase on your fitness monitor. You might even be thinking "OMG I have to present to these people?! Who even am I?"

But before you cue up the existential crisis, take a deep breath. You are in the right place, because guess what? WE ALL FEEL THIS WAY. All of us.

So now that you know you are in good company, tell that inner panicking voice to take a chill pill. Take another deep breath, grab a pen and paper and probably a highlighter too, and maybe a snack. I want you to relax because Sara is here to save the day, with a simple framework we can all use, for any scenario, that will have us all looking like professionals in no time! One more deep breath…and now turn the page, you've got this!

Melissa Seburg,
Senior Marketing Coordinator at TKDA

Melissa Seburg is a Senior Marketing Professional dedicated to the empowerment of leaders. Her success lies in her deliberate attention to the human experience of sharing a message. She believes great communication is the result of meaningful connection.

Leading from the front of the room with confidence is a continuous journey. At times you will find yourself making progress and other times you'll sense a never ending challenge. Remember to celebrate the wins and extend yourself compassion when needed. Keep going.

You got this!

Sara Krisher

01 Foundation

This chapter is full of strategies to boost your confidence and get you out of your own head.

"No matter what people tell you, words and ideas can change the world."

Robin Williams

BE BRAVE AND TAKE A STEP

Top 10 Biggest Fears

Speaking in public is always found on the list of top ten biggest fears. What happens in your body is a direct response to what is going on in your head.

It starts with what you're thinking and that's what informs your body to react. Pay attention to the thoughts racing through your mind before you present. Instead, choose empowering thoughts to replace the destructive ones.

"Feel the fear and do it anyway."
Susan Jeffers

Bravery and Fear

Being brave doesn't mean there is an absence of fear. Being brave means noticing the fear and taking action anyway. When you try something new it requires your personal power.

Learn what it feels like to act in the face of fear, nerves, and anxiety. As you get more familiar with the feelings you'll no longer see them as a threat, but rather an old friend that shows up to remind you this is something you care about.

Authentic Confidence

Authenticity means being real at the front of the room as well as in the hallway afterwards. Your audience needs you to be real if they are going to trust what you have to say.

 ProTip: Your audience wants you to succeed.

The Confidence Gap
by Russ Harris

The difficult thing about confidence building is at first you won't have confidence. There is a gap and Russ Harris wrote a book about it. He says the confidence gap is that space between where you are now and where you want to be.

CONFIDENCE NEEDS ACTION

» Waiting for confidence doesn't work.

» Confidence needs action.

» Begin taking bold steps in your life.

» Get familiar with the adrenaline surge that accompanies your action.

"A person often meets his destiny
on the road he took to avoid it."
Jean de La Fontaine

1. When have you done something scary?

2. What compelled you to take action?

3. What did you learn about yourself?

4. How can it inform what you are about to do?

"Everything you want is on the other side of fear."
Jack Canfield

20 CONFIDENCE BOOSTERS

Preparation for Speaking

1. Visualize Success. All the pros do it.
2. Memorize your start. A couple of sentences will do.
3. Be prepared and ready. Create a checklist.
4. Arrive early. Avoid the stress of being rushed.
5 Boost your luck. Superstitious? Wear your lucky socks.

Upon Arrival

6. Recognize exhilaration. The adrenaline rush isn't fear.
7. Be assured. You don't look as nervous as you feel.
8. Repeat a mantra. Interrupt a negative thought loop.
9. Be curious. Your personal power is in the present.
10. Stretch beforehand. It will calm your nerves.
11. Meet & greet. Recognize your audience as individuals.
12. Be gracious. Imagine you're a guest in their home.
13. Be optimistic. Everything could turn out great.
14. Get a look. Take in the view from the stage beforehand.

During

15. Take deep breaths. It slows your body's stress response.
16. STAND TALL. It sends signals to your brain that you are ready.
17. Get grounded. Take a deep breath before you begin.
18. Take it in. Recognize the energy from the audience.
19. Laugh at yourself. Nobody is perfect.
20. Remember to smile. It's a privilege to speak.

My Confidence Boosting Strategy:

NICE TO MEET YOU

No doubt you've been asked to introduce yourself many times throughout your career. Although it seems like a very simple task, it can be the beginning of an anxiety spiral.

When you know how to express who you are and what you do succinctly you'll be ready to do it at a moment's notice with confidence.

Example
Name: Sara Krisher
Company: STAND TALL
Is: a confidence building company
Does: Training and coaching
Means: Leaders can lead at the front of the room with CONFIDENCE

Putting it all together…
"I'm Sara Krisher, the owner of a confidence building company called STAND TALL. I teach leaders to rid themselves of fear, so they can lead at the front of the room with CONFIDENCE."

Your Intro
Name:
_____
Company:
_____
Is:
_____
Does:
_____
Means:
_____
Putting it all together…
_____

"Is, Does, Means" structure, created by Steve Kloyda, The Prospecting Expert.

PERSONAL SPEAKING ASSESSMENT
Technical Skills

Date: _____

Rate yourself on each of the below. 1=Needs work 5=Nailed it

Eye Contact Make eye contact with your audience like you would a trusted friend.	1	2	3	4	5
Gestures Freely using your hands to communicate what you are saying.	1	2	3	4	5
Movement Move purposefully with comfort.	1	2	3	4	5
Language Speaking clearly and using words the audience understands.	1	2	3	4	5
Fillers (umm...) Comfortable with pauses and your transitions flow. No nervous fillers.	1	2	3	4	5
Pace Speaking pace is authentic to you. You like to slow down or pause for emphasis.	1	2	3	4	5
Pause Comfortable with silence and you breathe naturally.	1	2	3	4	5
Projection Your volume is audible to the front and back row.	1	2	3	4	5
Tone Using the full range of your voice with variety as you would talking to a friend.	1	2	3	4	5

NOTES

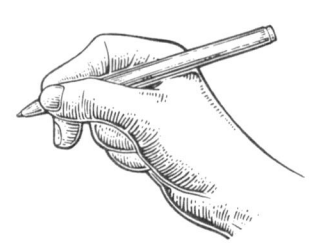

PERSONAL SPEAKING ASSESSMENT
Overall Impression

Rate yourself on each of the below. 1=Needs work   5=Nailed it

Approachability Inviting, friendly, and interested in your audience.	1	2	3	4	5
Confidence Bring your whole self to the front of the room and know your message is of value.	1	2	3	4	5
Authenticity You are the same off stage as you are on stage.	1	2	3	4	5
Credibility You are respected for your experience and know your subject matter.	1	2	3	4	5
Passionate You care about your topic. It's communicated in what you say and how you say it.	1	2	3	4	5
Engagement You find ways to interact with your audience.	1	2	3	4	5
Main Point Your message is understood and the audience walks away knowing what it was all for.	1	2	3	4	5
Timing You know how much time you have to speak and start and end on time.	1	2	3	4	5

NOTES

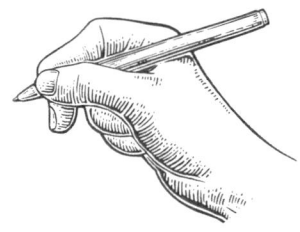

Captivate Your Audience • 21

WHAT'S THE BIGGER REASON?

When you know the purpose behind what you're doing it gives your desire some weight. It will lead you to try once more when you otherwise want to give up.

Resilience Statements	Write it in your own words.
☐ I am meant to be a better leader. ☐ I want others to take me seriously. ☐ I want to make a big impact. ☐ I want to advance in my career. ☐ I am meant to influence with my words. ☐ I have a meaningful message to share. ☐ I want to be recognized publicly. ☐ I want to change hearts and minds. ☐ I must conquer my fear. ☐ I want to be admired. ☐ _____	

Tacit versus explicit

Tacit knowledge is not easily passed on. It involves your experience, education, skillset, talents, and unique view. You are asked to present because you have tacit knowledge only you can share.

If you were asked to simply pass along information that would be explicit knowledge and could easily be sent in an email. Never underestimate the power of you.

"Tacit knowledge is like teaching someone to ride a bike. It requires more than the written word."

Sara Krisher

The Impact of You

Above all else, be yourself. When you speak you don't need to be like anyone else. The magic you hold is *being you*.

"Courage is contagious.
Every time we choose courage, we make everyone around us a little better and the world a little braver."
Brene Brown

The Power of Vulnerability

Brene Brown is a research professor who studies vulnerability and courage. She is a best selling author and delivered one of the most popular TED Talks of all time.

Check it out: https://www.ted.com/talks/brene_brown_on_vulnerability

02 Preparation

This chapter is jam packed full of tips and tools to ready your mind and understand your audience.

"Uncertainty is the root of all progress and all growth. As the old adage goes, the man who believes he knows everything learns nothing. We cannot learn anything without first not knowing something."

Mark Manson

WHAT'S THE GOAL?

Focus on your Audience

Your audience has a unique experience, a specific perspective, and personal involvement in your topic. The collective knowledge sitting in front of you is brilliant. Sharing your message with them is a privilege.

Focus on connecting with your audience and make your presentation audience-centric. You'll feel better because you'll be focused on them and not yourself. They'll feel acknowledged and interested in hearing what you have to say.

You Have Credibility

As a vetted speaker at the front of the room you already have the distinct credit of having some authority on the topic you're speaking about. There is no need to flood the audience with your intelligence or share your credentials at length. You already have the credibility of an expert, instead focus on being approachable.

Be Approachable

Being approachable allows the audience the space to be curious and thoughtful. They will approach you afterwards and be a valuable part of a continuing conversation.

If the audience feels it's safe to approach you afterwards they will share with you what resonated most or what they are struggling to understand. You'll become a better speaker if you hear what your audience is telling you.

BE KIND TO YOU

Self-compassion is extending compassion to one's self in instances of perceived inadequacy, failure, or general suffering. Having compassion for yourself means that you honor and accept your humanness. It means you treat yourself as you would a good friend.[1]

[1]Adapted from Dr. Kristin Neff's definition - self-compassion.org

Power Pose for more Confidence

It's comforting to know that even when we forget to extend ourselves compassion we can still boost our confidence by choosing how we hold our body. Amy Cuddy, Social Psychologist, describes how body language doesn't only influence how others perceive you, but can also play into how your see yourself. Watch Amy's TED Talk, *Your body language shapes who you are*, to learn about the "power pose" to boost your confidence.

https://www.ted.com/talks/amy_cuddy_your_body_language_shapes_who_you_are

What do you believe about your audience?

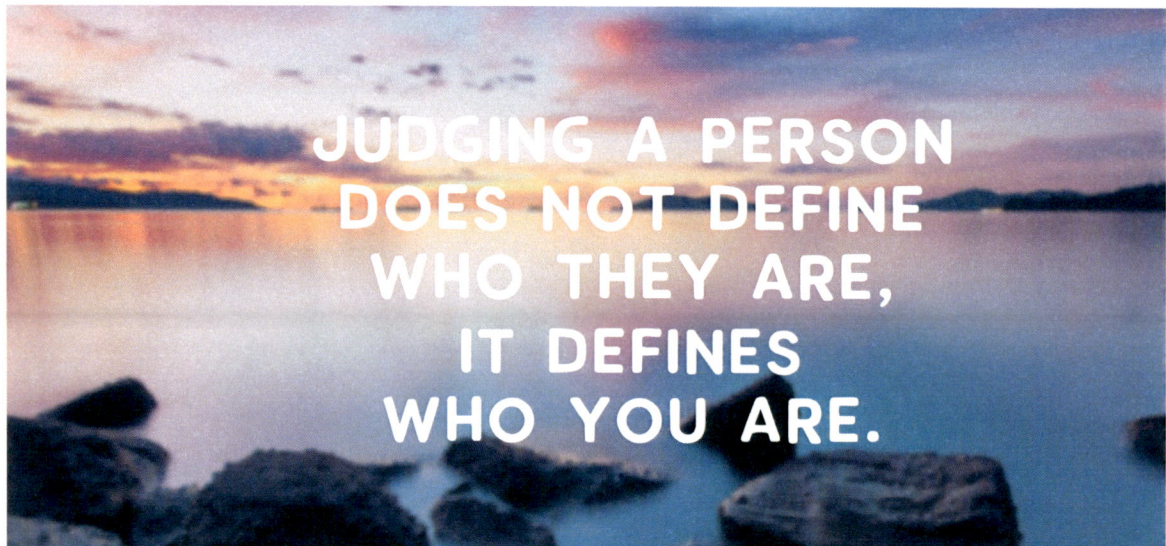

When a leader makes their way to the front of the room they aim to make a difference and affect lives or situations for the better. They don't always consider how they feel about their audience and what they believe about them.

Have you ever sat through a presentation where you've felt like you'd been talked down to, made fun of, or even yelled at by the presenter? Maybe you didn't put words to it, but left the presentation feeling depressed, defeated, or angry. If you've ever walked away feeling worse for having shared your time with a presenter, you'll understand the importance of this next exercise.

Our mentality, as a presenter, is something we carry with us and it gets delivered in what we say and how we say it whether we like it or not.

For example, if you believe your audience is helpless and dumb and needs you in order to make it through life you will inevitably treat them like idiots. Your arrogance will be off putting, and your message will be difficult to grasp. You might have the solution for world peace, but if you don't believe your audience is capable, they will either prove you right or be so irritated with you they'll want to run out kicking and screaming.

GETTING TO KNOW YOUR AUDIENCE

Take some time to answer the questions below.

Keep in mind, when your audience sees you as a champion of their success they want more of you.

Who is your audience?

_____

What do you know about them?

_____

What are their challenges or struggles?

_____

What does your audience need or desire?

_____

What gets in the way of them having what they need or desire?

_____

What can your audience do to overcome the obstacles and have what they desire?

_____

What makes you care?

_____

What experience do you have with their challenge?

_____

What will you do to serve them or help them overcome their challenge?

_____

Captivate Your Audience • 29

03 Creation

In this chapter you'll learn to masterfully design your speeches with the 7Cs framework.

"When seen through a wider lens, creativity is not simply 'the arts', it is a natural state and condition that arises in all human beings when their level of fear is diminshed."

Peter Himmelman

The Creative Process

Writing a speech is a creative process. The basic structure of a speech includes an intro, body and close. You have as much freedom as you'd like in how you pull your content together. Because this is a creative process it can be very uncomfortable at first.

Just like when a painter puts a brush to the canvas without knowing how the final product will look, you will need to trust that your words will turn into art in the end.

It's completely acceptable to be messy. When you work through your speech verbally you'll refine your talk. The messy creative process will sort its way out. You'll begin to see clearly what needs to be included and what can be tossed out.

A Simple Framework

Typing out a presentation ensures you will be tethered to a script. Step away from writing and sketch a path instead.

Create your presentation with the 7C's Framework

- Save yourself time creating your presentation
- Create an organized storyline
- Minimize overthinking and over analyzing
- Easily remember what to say under pressure

"No matter how much you yearn to do everything flawlessly, the stage will teach you humility."

Sara Krisher

7 C's to Create Content

Critical Point
What is the one thing you need to convey? Make it easy to remember. This is your guide for determining what you share.

Captivate
Captivate them right away. These are the first words out of your mouth so get them interested. Make it intriguing and relevant.

Connect
Introduce yourself and establish a relationship with your audience. The goal is to find a way to relate to your audience.

Consensus
Think of this as setting the agenda, but get your audience involved. Share what's next and ask them to share why it's important.

Core
Choose three core ideas that will support your critical point and make it make sense to your audience by categorizing your stories, research and activities accordingly.

Commitment
Now is the time to ask your audience to do something. Give feedback, take one step, approach you afterwards, etc.

Conclusion
Focus on your critical point and if possible, wrap up all you've shared with a final story. Leave them inspired to act.

www.STANDTALL-LLC.com

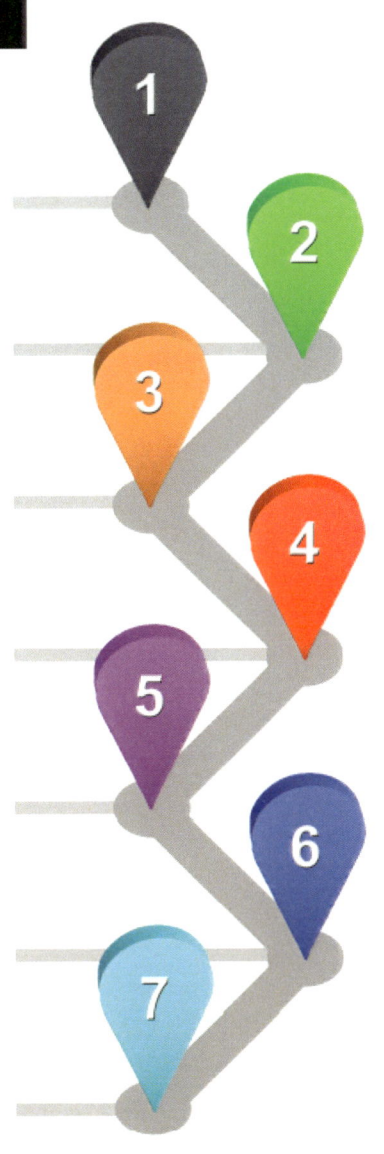

Lead From The Front of The Room With **CONFIDENCE**

©STAND TALL 2018

THE 7Cs WORKSHEET

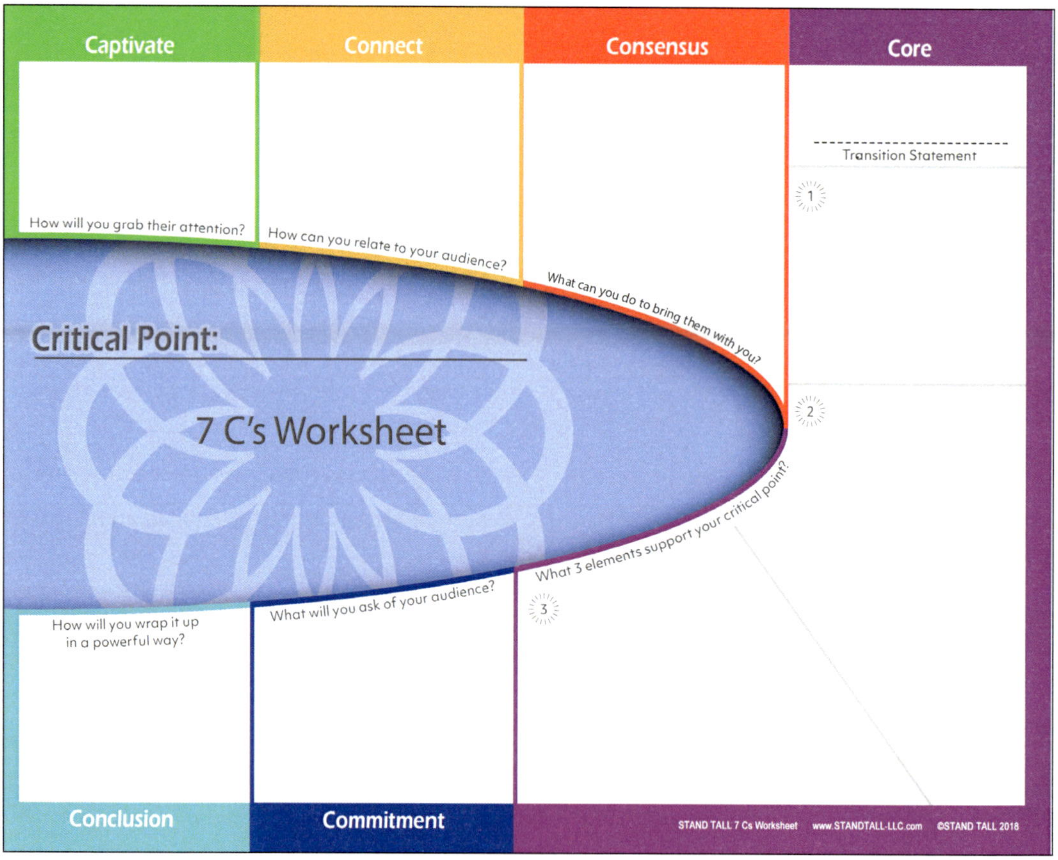

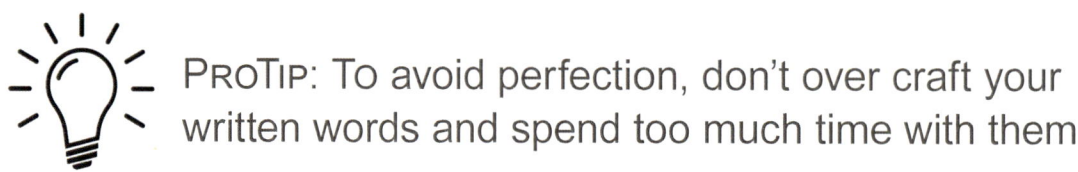

PROTIP: To avoid perfection, don't over craft your written words and spend too much time with them.

Create a visual map for yourself by using the 7C's worksheet. Draw images to represent stories and concepts. Practice your talk using your visual map.

This allows you to create a path for your talk as well as develop multiple options to communicate your message. You'll develop flexibility and creativity. If you are doing this correctly you won't say your presentation twice the same way.

Sara Krisher • 36

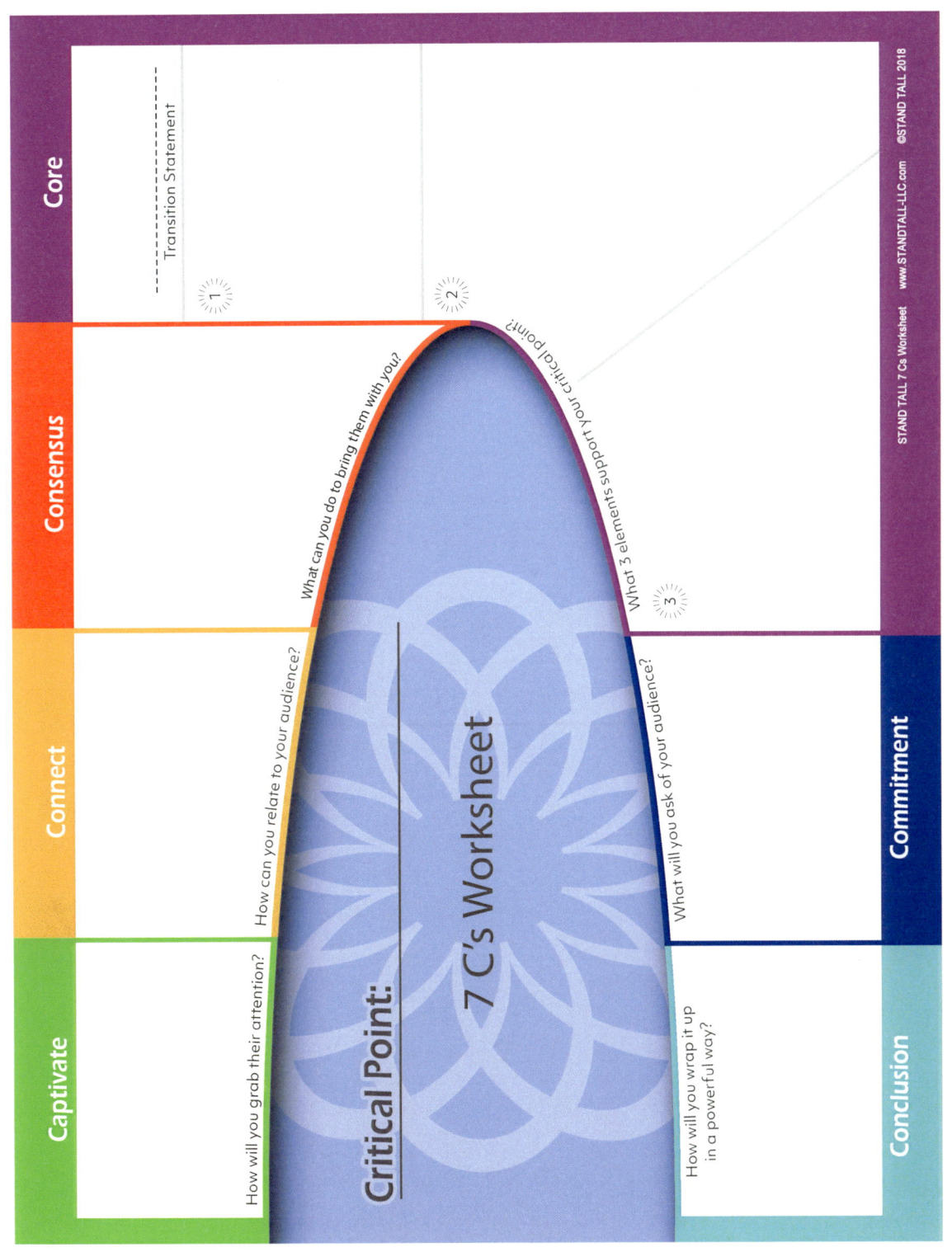

7 C's Worksheet

Critical Point: _____

Captivate
How will you grab their attention?

Connect
How can you relate to your audience?

Consensus
What can you do to bring them with you?

Core
Transition Statement
1.
2.
What 3 elements support your critical point?
3.

Commitment
What will you ask of your audience?

Conclusion
How will you wrap it up in a powerful way?

STAND TALL 7 Cs Worksheet • ©STAND TALL 2018 • www.STANDTALL-LLC.com

Captivate Your Audience • 37

GETTING STARTED

Example of the 7's Worksheet

Draw Pictures ~ Use Color ~ Clockwise Direction

Visual Mapping Method

This is an example of a simple visual map. You can apply this technique to a short presentation or a long one. Try it out and 'see' the impact it has on your confidence level.

When you can draw your visual map from memory without looking at your first drawing you will be able to remember it under pressure. A longer speech may require you to draw the visual map multiple times before you commit it to memory.

Starting From Scratch

When you're creating a presentation from scratch, start with a brain dump. Think of anything you can possibly imagine that has anything to do with your topic and don't judge it. Once you've exhausted all of your ideas take a look at what you have in front of you.

Now, take three different colored highlighters and try to group everything you've written into three parts. Those parts may turn into the core of your presentation.

Take a close look. Are there any patterns that emerge? Are there any sequences?

For example, if you see there is a clear order for sharing the information on your topic you may want to consider a chronological structure. For more ideas for your core check out the possible speaking structures page.

1. Critical Point

What one thing does the audience need to walk away knowing?

The Critical Point is the main point of your speech. It's the reason you spent hours preparing and it's the reason the audience will go home thinking differently. The Critical Point needs to drive your presentation. It's powerful if it's tweetable. If you're able to keep it short and memorable it will stick with your audience. You'll want to say your Critical Point multiple times throughout your speech for emphasis. It's what you want them to walk away with at the end of your presentation. You'll want to develop your Critical Point first in your content development. It will keep you focused and on point throughout the process.

Clear - Memorable - Audience Centric

My Critical Point is...

```
┌─────────────────────────────────────────────────┐
│                                                 │
│                                                 │
│    Example: "Don't leave home without it." American Express │
└─────────────────────────────────────────────────┘
```

Sara Krisher • 40

INSIGHTS

"If you are always trying to be normal you will never know how amazing you can be."

Maya Angelou

Taming your Gremlin

by Rick Carson

Want to stop the mean voice in your head that sabotages your efforts? Check this book out. It'll have you creating a new dialogue that supports you instead of destroying your self-confidence.

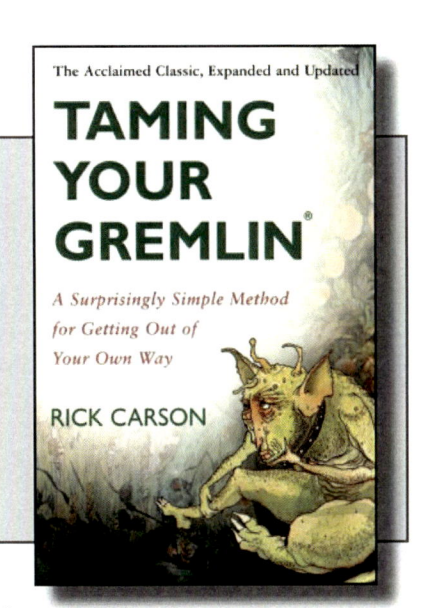

2. Captivate

Find a way to relate to your audience.

Try starting with a personal story related to your main point. It will make you feel confident because you lived it, you don't have to work hard to remember it, and it gets you focused on relating to the audience.

Your captivating story can be thirty seconds to a minute. It doesn't have to be very long. Be sure to tie it to your critical point.

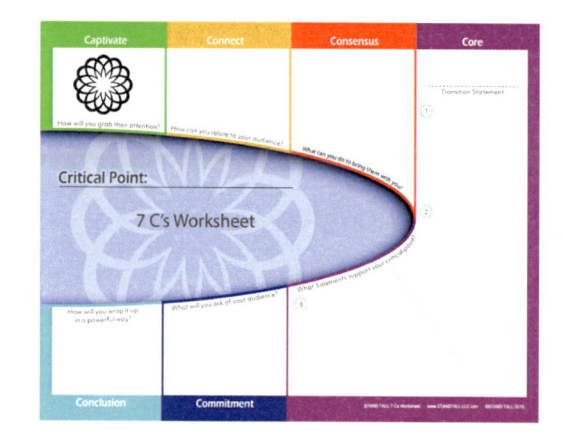

Write your ideas here:

You may find it useful to complete this section after you develop the core.

3. Connect

How can you relate to your audience?

After you open your speech by captivating them, you'll want to connect with your audience. Find a way to relate to them. If they know you are like them they will want to hear what you have to say.

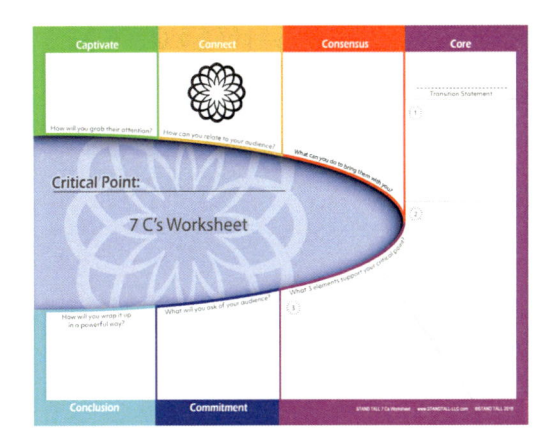

THOUGHT STARTERS

How are you like your audience?

Have you been in their shoes before?

How can you connect with them?

Consider sharing these ideas:

1. Introduce yourself in an approachable way.

2. How can you relate to your audience?

3. Share why you care about your topic or subject matter.

Captivate Your Audience • 43

BE RELATABLE

Connect with your audience

If you connect with your audience, they'll care about what you say. To connect, make the topic you're speaking about relevant and relatable with stories. If you make the stories personal, the audience feels like they know you!

smile

PROTIP: Smile because it puts others at ease and it's a non-verbal invitation for your audience to approach you.

SHARING WISDOM

Use this three part structure anytime throughout your presentation.

1 Challenge Faced
What is the problem or challenge?

2 Decision Made
What decision was made?

3 Lesson Learned
What was the lesson learned?

Stories boost confidence

When we're talking to our coworkers, friends or family about something we experienced earlier in the day, we connect naturally. We know instinctually that stories are a great way to make our point, share something important, or engage someone.

Stories help us connect and remember a lesson long after a speech is over. Stories are interesting, significant, and reveal wisdom. It's easy to remember how to tell a story because there is a clear beginning, middle, and end. There is no fear of forgetting and that can calm some nerves!

4. Consensus

What can you do to bring your audience along with you?

Consensus is a general agreement about something: an idea or opinion that is shared by all the people in a group.

Try asking a question to discover what makes this topic important to your audience.

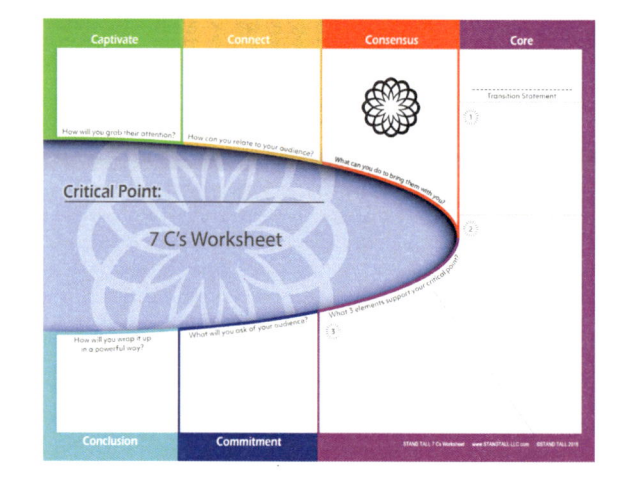

What makes this important to you?

5. Core

How can you support your critical point?

The purpose of your speech is to have your audience hear and understand your message. Whether you are trying to educate, persuade, or motivate you'll still need to be heard.

Try creating three core ideas to support your critical point. Make it audience-centric and keep it simple for greater impact.

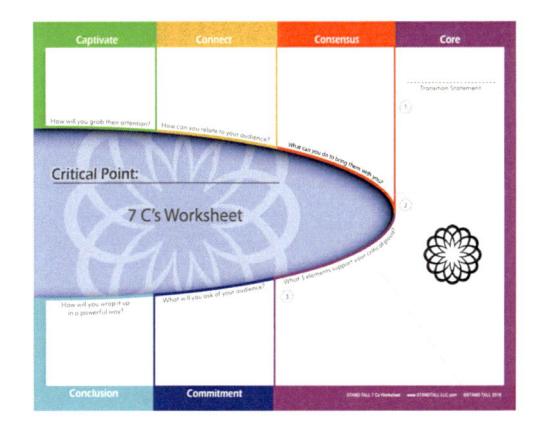

What three core ideas can prove or support your Critical Point?

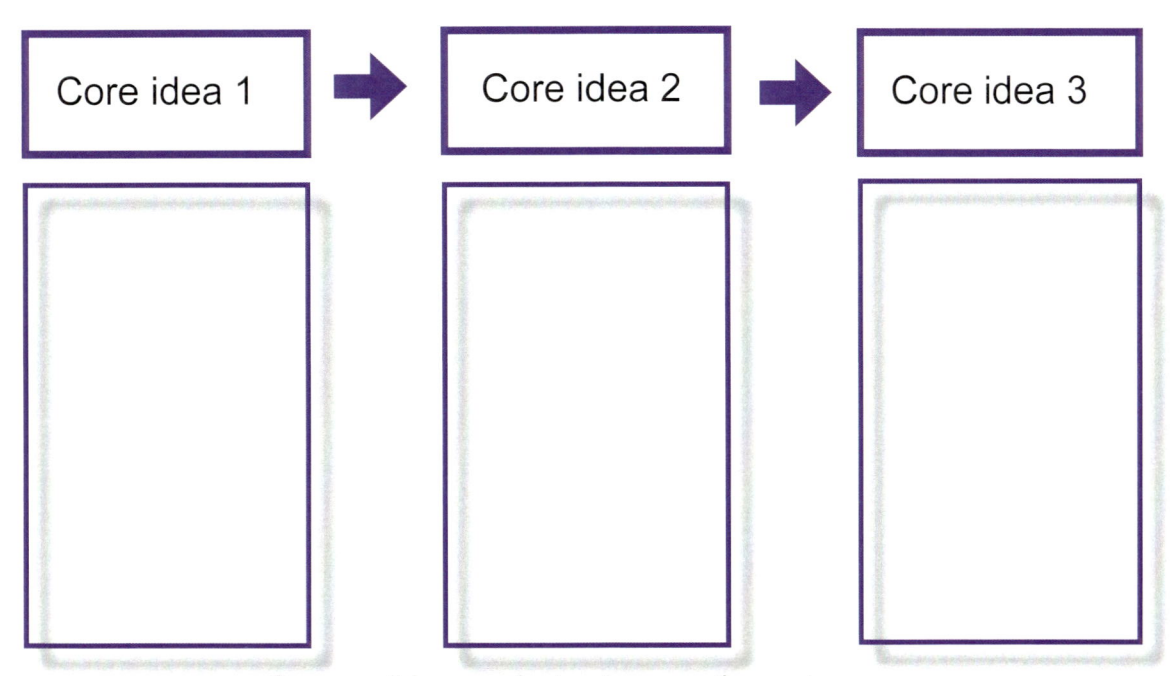

| Core idea 1 | ➡ | Core idea 2 | ➡ | Core idea 3 |

See possible speech structures on the next page.
Captivate Your Audience • 47

POSSIBLE SPEECH STRUCTURES

Choose a structure for your core.

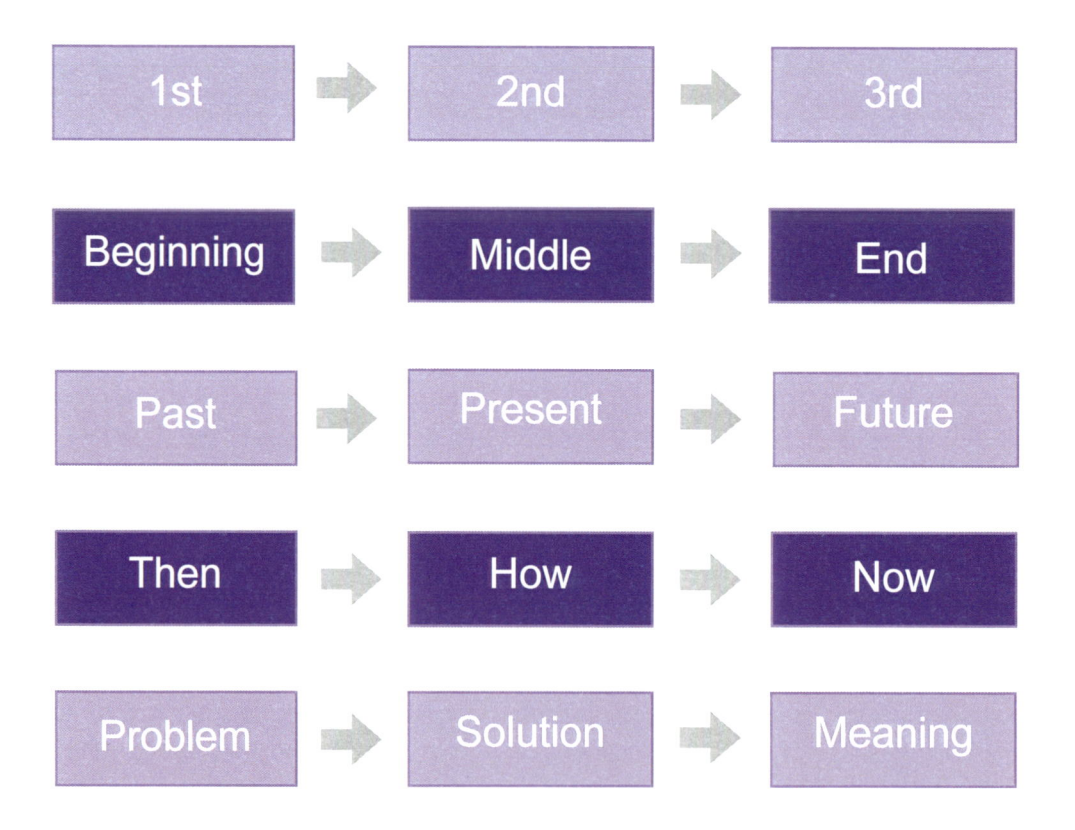

1st	➡	2nd	➡	3rd
Beginning	➡	Middle	➡	End
Past	➡	Present	➡	Future
Then	➡	How	➡	Now
Problem	➡	Solution	➡	Meaning

Or try using 3 of something.

The 3 most important factors are…

The 3 biggest reasons are…

The 3 ways to overcome this are…

My 3 favorites on this list are…

The 3 traps to look out for are…

The 3 problems we face are…

Expand Your Core Ideas

Expand your core ideas using evidence or proof. Take a look at the list provided and add some of your own. Be sure to consider how much time you have to speak when determining which proof points, you will choose.

Proof Points

CHOOSE ONE OR MANY TO EXPAND YOUR CORE IDEAS

- ☐ Activities
- ☐ Article
- ☐ Book
- ☐ Case study
- ☐ Example
- ☐ Facts
- ☐ Historical reference
- ☐ Illustration
- ☐ Letter
- ☐ Projections
- ☐ Quote
- ☐ Research study
- ☐ Social Proof
- ☐ Statistics
- ☐ Story
- ☐ Survey
- ☐ Video
- ☐ Other

Transition Statement

Include a transition statement that introduces your core. This will give your audience a preview of what's to come.

Write your ideas here:

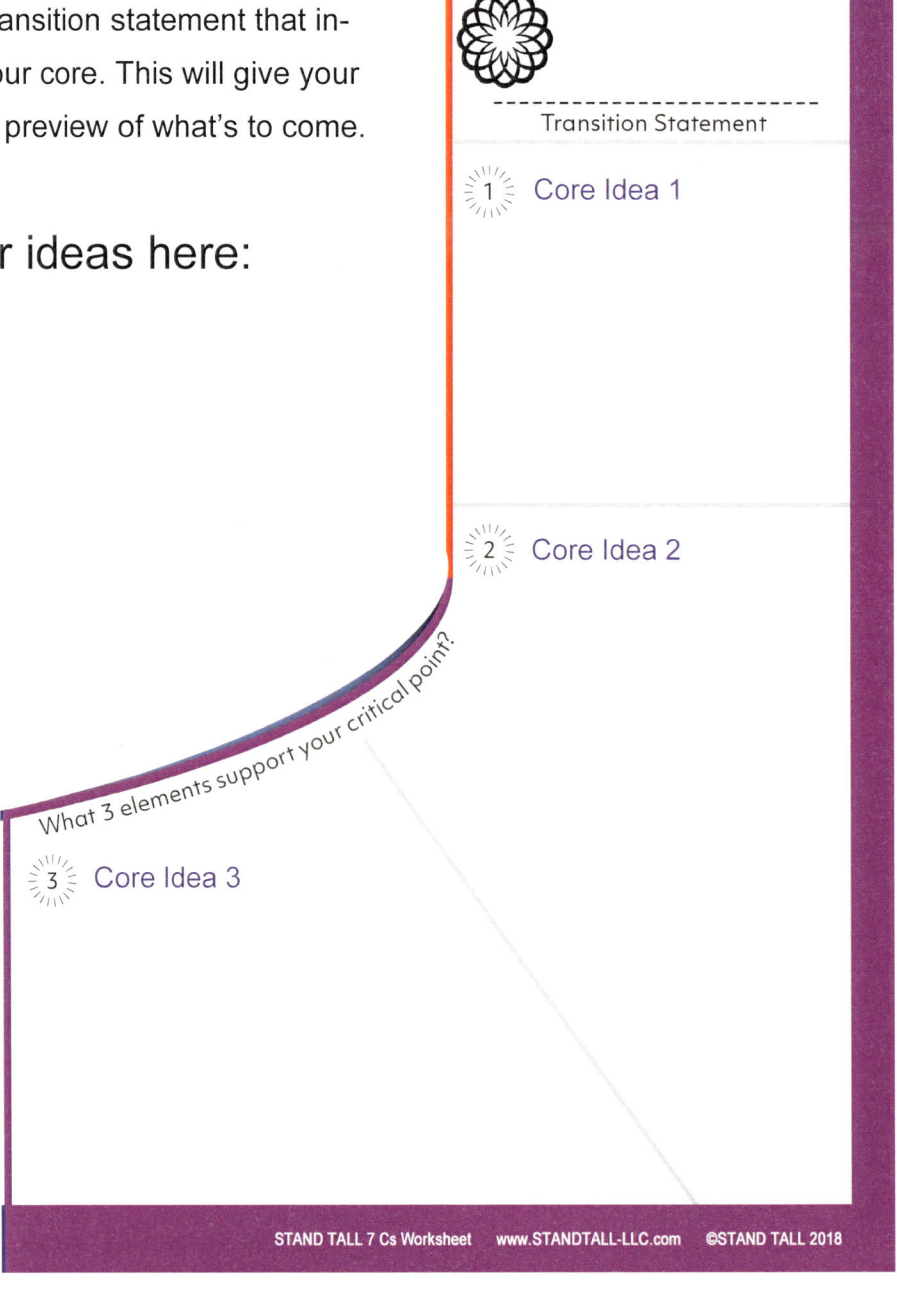

Core

Transition Statement

1 Core Idea 1

2 Core Idea 2

What 3 elements support your critical point?

3 Core Idea 3

STAND TALL 7 Cs Worksheet   www.STANDTALL-LLC.com   ©STAND TALL 2018

6. Commitment

What will you ask of your audience?

This is your chance to tell your audience what you want from them. Do you want them to take some kind of action? Do you want them to think differently?

Make sure it's this clear. If you want their feedback ask them. If you want them to engage with you afterwards now is your chance to make this known.

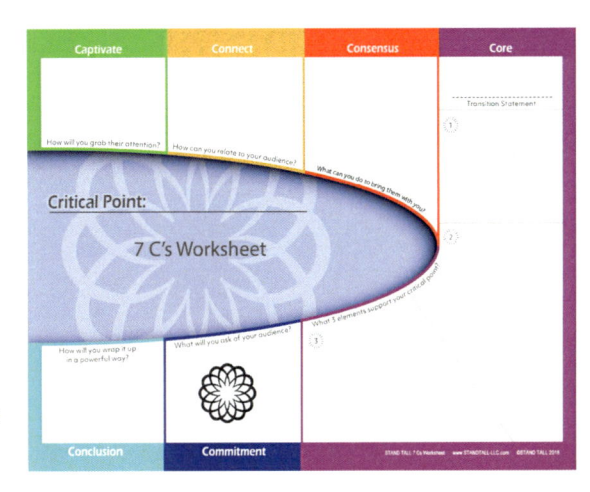

The commitment I want from my audience:

Captivate Your Audience • 51

7. Conclusion

How can you wrap it all together in a powerful way?

Your conclusion is most powerful if it ties your critical point and your captivating intro into a nice story. A story that drives your point home is going to leave them with a completed feeling.

How do you want them to feel at the end of your presentation?

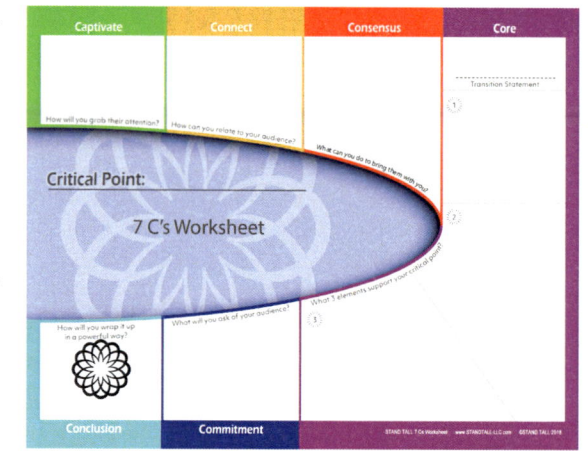

A Great Conclusion

» Provides a vision of what's possible

» Motivates and inspires

» Connects on a personal level

» Invites action

» Feels complete

04 Connection

The focus of this chapter is fostering interaction with your audience by creating an experience that involves their input.

"Normal and average are plain and boring. Special and different is exciting and sets you apart."

Danika Socwell

BE ENGAGING

Two-way communication is critical for any presenter today. Audiences no longer have the attention spans they once had. Great orators of the past never had to compete with the ever-enticing hand-held technology and demands of today.

Audience Engagement is the extent to which the audience is interested or actively involved with your message.

You can engage your audience with tools beyond your voice. Create a full experience by using visuals such as pictures or slides and activities that may involve games or asking for volunteers. Also consider the environment. How is the room laid out, is there flow, is the lighting appropriate for your presentation? Combine those with your powerful voice that comes to life through stories and humor and you're setup for a great event.

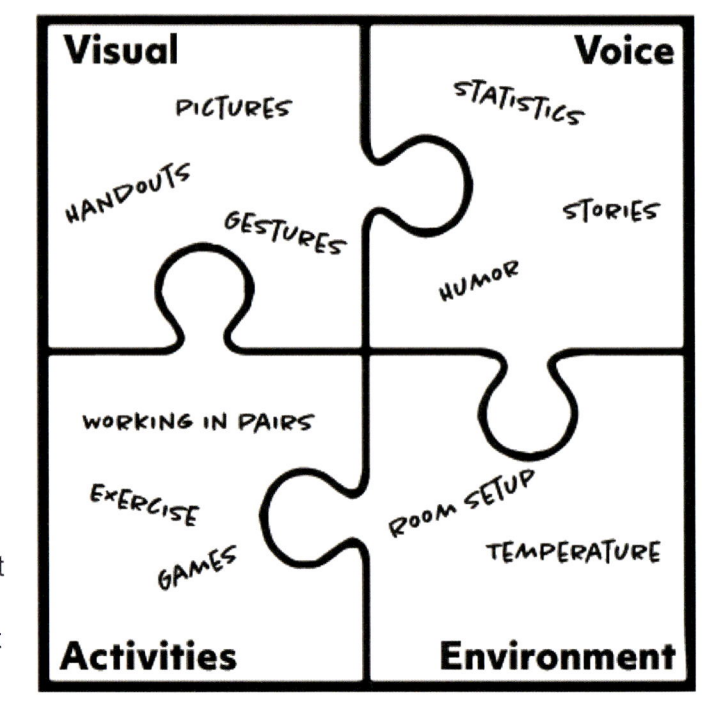

Visual: Pictures, Handouts, Gestures

Voice: Statistics, Stories, Humor

Activities: Working in Pairs, Exercise, Games

Environment: Room Setup, Temperature

Sara Krisher • 54

How Will You Engage?

Audience engagement is one of the keys to making your message heard. What engagement ideas will you use to create an experience for your audience?

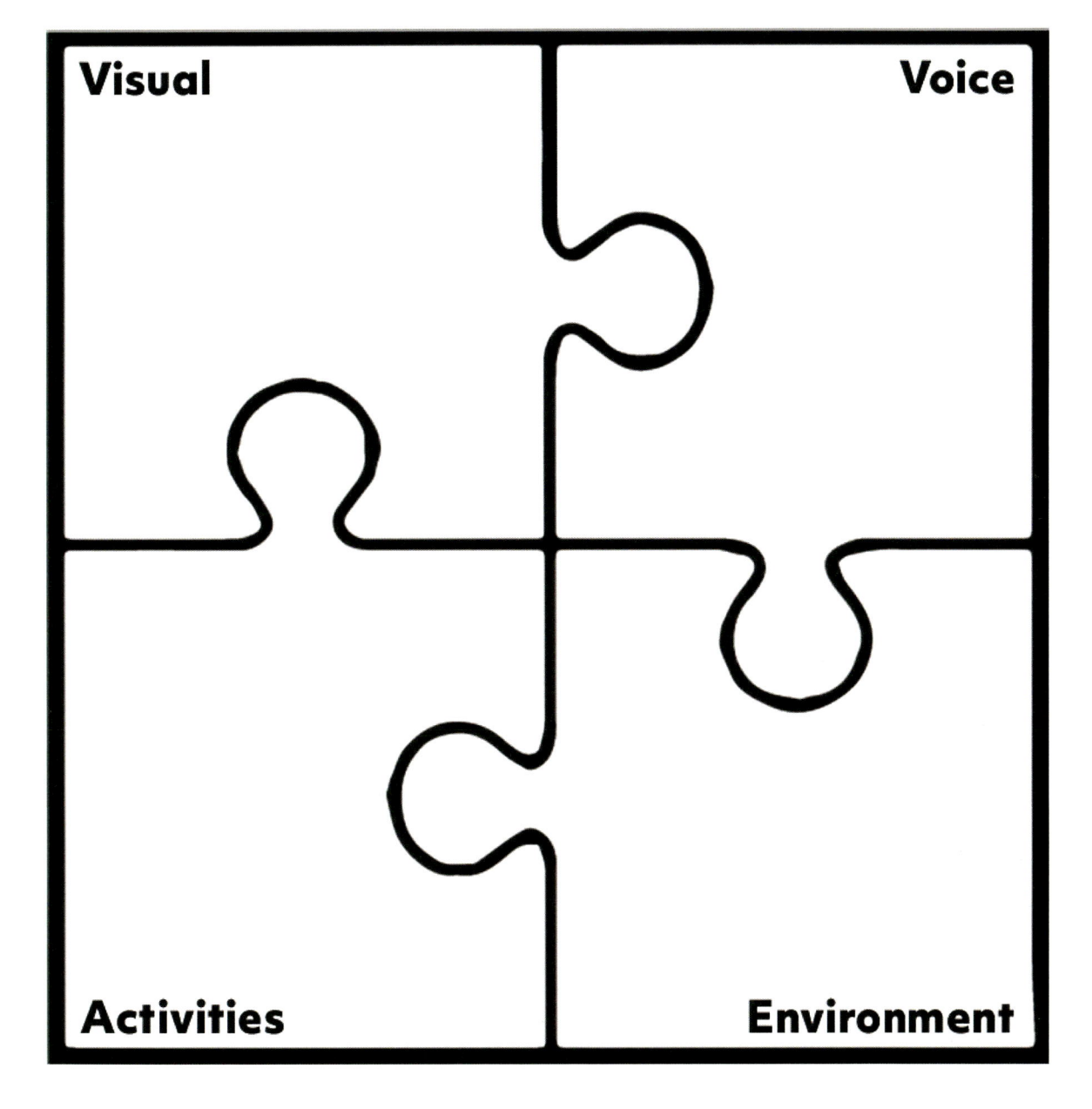

Visual	**Voice**
Activities	**Environment**

Captivate Your Audience • 55

Engage Your Audience Virtually

- ☐ Acknowledgement by name
- ☐ Allow space for contemplation
- ☐ Bring some energy
- ☐ Change it up
- ☐ Create a unified experience
- ☐ Create relevant activities
- ☐ Encourage gestures (thumbs up)
- ☐ Engage their senses
- ☐ Have a drawing for a prize
- ☐ Have fun
- ☐ Incorporate movement
- ☐ Incorporate writing
- ☐ Introduce a prop
- ☐ Invite all the voices in the room
- ☐ Leverage the unexpected
- ☐ Make the subject matter personal
- ☐ Play games
- ☐ Play off each other (round robin)
- ☐ Practice eye contact
- ☐ Provide a worksheet
- ☐ Recall memories
- ☐ Recognize accomplishments
- ☐ Refer to an article
- ☐ Request cameras be turned on
- ☐ Require prework
- ☐ Rock, paper, scissors to decide
- ☐ Share lessons learned
- ☐ Share stories
- ☐ Show a video
- ☐ Smile often
- ☐ Tap into creativity
- ☐ Type in the chat box
- ☐ Use breakout rooms
- ☐ Use conversational language
- ☐ Use metaphors to explain
- ☐ Use polling feature
- ☐ Use relevant examples
- ☐ Wait for answers to questions
- ☐ Work towards a common goal

How to Connect Virtually

1. Know the Critical Point
The Critical Point is the one thing you want them to walk away knowing. In any communication it can be easy to get off track or meander while sharing a message. Prepare a critical point in advance so you stay the course and share it with your audience, so they understand the purpose and context of the meeting.

2. Invite a conversation
Plan a few questions in advance. Your audience will appreciate a less formal tone and an opportunity to be a part of the discussion. Ask a question and get your audience to give input in the first ten minutes so they remain active listeners not passive listeners.

3. Check in often
Whether in-person or virtual, if you are presenting information, you'll want to check in with your audience to determine if they are listening and understanding what you're sharing. A check in could be a question like, 'What questions do you have?' or 'What isn't making sense?' Everyone learns differently so don't take offense if they don't get it right away.

4. Involve them in the learning
A great way to keep your audience engaged and connected is to have them work in teams or individually to experience the learning. Consider that the audio channel (or speaking only) is just one-way people learn. Another way they learn is by doing. How can you involve them in the doing? In a virtual setting you can whiteboard as a group, you can get into break out rooms for mini discussions, and you can email handouts to work on during the meeting.

5. Pay attention to nuances
You've probably noticed nuances during your in-person meetings without even trying. Maybe you saw your audience shift back in their seats and fold their arms. You sensed they weren't buying what you were selling so you changed up your approach. In a virtual meeting you can still tap into these subtleties. Don't be afraid to ask about the temperature in the room. (metaphorically of course)

Virtual Presentation Cheat Sheet

What to avoid as a Presenter:

- Technology issues, internet problems, or other glitches
- No familiarity with the platform being used (Zoom, Google Meets, Webex etc)
- Participants being unengaged or leave early
- No moderator to assist with chat, muting, and questions
- Taking too long to get to the point
- Assuming participants know how you want them to engage

What to avoid as a Participant:

- Background noises
- Unprofessional background
- Technology issues, internet problems, or other glitches
- No familiarity or understanding of the virtual platform
- Distractions, multi-tasking, and/or traveling
- Turning off your video (unless tech issues prevent you from having it on)
- Thinking that your contribution doesn't matter or that you won't be missed
- Chat discussions that aren't productive or positive

METAPHORS

A metaphor states one thing is another thing, which is not literally true, but helps explain a concept in a simple way.

You've heard the saying "a picture is worth a thousand words". There are many ways to skin a cat, but metaphors are an incredibly effective way to drive your point home. Metaphors give you the ability to make a profound impression with very few words.

If you are in sales, an example of a metaphor you might use is "my sales skyrocketed last month" or "this week my numbers tanked". If you're talking to your client you might say "I understand your concerns, you're stranded in the Sahara right now and our systems address this very issue."

STORYTELLING

Sharing a story is a great way to make a point. Being a great story teller is a learned skill. To get started, draw from your own experiences and share stories from your life. This is a great way to make a connection with your audience. Be careful not to make yourself the hero of your story. Instead, make your client or audience the hero.

A story is compelling when it:

- » Provides context or setup
- » Introduces a problem or challenge
- » Easy to understand
- » Drives home a point you are making

"Every story needs a point and every point needs a story."
Unknown

Sara Krisher • 60

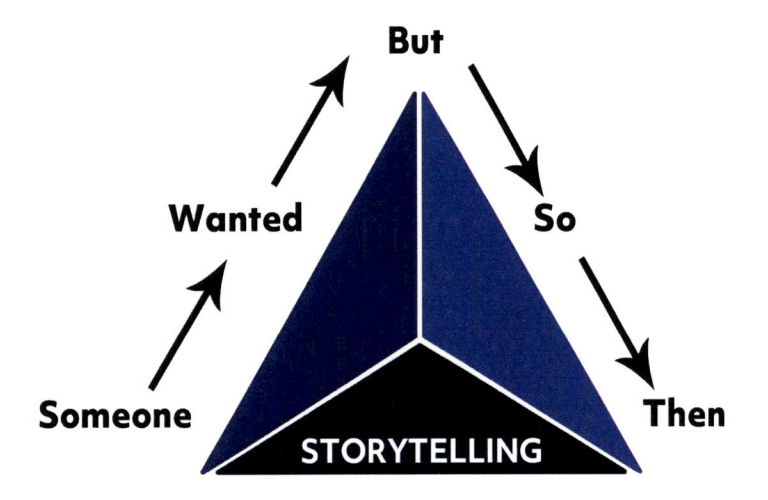

Share a story using the Someone - Wanted - But - So - Then formula. Consider your audience and make sure they know what point you are trying to make with your story. Have fun!

Someone

Who is the main character?

Wanted

What did the character want?

But

What was the problem?

So

How did the character try to solve the problem?

Then

What was the resolution to the problem?

What Makes a Great Presenter?

A great speaker is not remembered for his or her technical speaking skills. Instead, it is the powerful message we remember. Sometimes we don't even remember what was said, but rather how we felt. We walk away as an audience member saying, "That was a great presentation!"

As an audience member we don't always notice the presenter had great eye contact, or paused at just the right time, or that their gestures were timely and meaningful. We don't notice because we are not distracted by poor speaking habits. Had their speech been littered with ums and ahs we may not have felt the incredible power of the message. This is why it's important to break down the technical aspects of a solid presentation and get good at it. If we don't do the work we'll find our message is lost, or our audience is disengaged, and our efforts were futile.

The Art of Speaking

Will Stephen demonstrates the art of speaking by spending an entire speech saying nothing, while demonstrating how the use of voice, pace, and drama can make a person sound really interesting. Watch his TEDx Talk and see what you can learn.

How to sound smart in your TEDx Talk | Will Stephen | TEDxNewYork
https://www.youtube.com/watch?v=8S0FDjFBj8o&vl=en

Six Connection Points

1. **SMILE** because it disarms your audience and you look like you are enjoying your time with them.

2. **EYE CONTACT** shows you're not scared and promotes trust so the audience has confidence in your message.

3. **ACKNOWLEDGE** your audience and show them you care by asking questions, answering questions, commenting on their interests, or including their concerns in your talk.

4. **PASSION** for your message shows you care, evokes emotion and impacts hearts and minds.

5. **STORIES** make your message more relatable and easier to remember.

6. **BE YOU** because the audience loves a real person speaking to them and there is no perfect presenter.

Practice

ProTip: Memorize your opening sentences to get you started smoothly.

If you have the opportunity to practice in front of a live audience, you'll want to do it. Nothing beats the energy and feedback of a live audience. What makes you a great writer doesn't make you a great speaker.

The written word and spoken word are two completely different modalities. The words you wrote that were so expertly chosen become nearly impossible to retrieve while speaking. If writing is a part of your preparation process you'll be wise to step away from the writing as soon as possible and begin practicing your speech out loud with your visual map. Get comfortable delivering your message different each time.

Start with Confidence

Having trouble remembering how you were going to start? Begin your story with one of the story ramps below or create your own. Memorizing your start will ease you into your story with confidence.

Story Ramps

There I was…

It wasn't long ago…

I still remember…

I was on high alert when…

How could I have known…

I was at a crossroads…

Reflecting on the past week…

I could tell this day was different…

The hair on the back of my neck stood straight up…

She looked at me and, in that moment, …

ELEMENTS OF AUDIENCE ENGAGEMENT

Invite Voices Early

The sooner you get the audience responding to you the better. As soon as a voice is allowed to show up in the room, others will feel permitted to contribute. It will encourage audience engagement throughout your presentation.

Ask and Wait

When you ask a question of your audience, wait for the answer. If you don't you'll set up a passive listening audience. They will assume you don't want their feedback. It'll make it extremely difficult to involve them in activities later in your presentation. There is no right answer to how long you should wait. It's longer than you think. Try waiting until there is an answer. It may feel awkward, but someone will always speak up. Believe that and it will be true.

Yes, and...

Sometimes you'll ask a question of the audience and you'll get a response you didn't anticipate. It's best to remain open and allow for all kinds of answers. Work with what is said and dignify their answer. The worst thing you can do is make them feel wrong for having contributed. It will shut down others and your audience participation will be nearly impossible.

Audience is the Hero

Never embarrass or talk down to your audience. Treat them like the smart capable people they are, or they will know instantly. Your audience should always be the hero in examples and stories. Allow them to be the star because it empowers them to take action. If you must have a volunteer allow them to raise their hand. Don't select a volunteer that hasn't expressed interest.

ELEMENTS OF AUDIENCE ENGAGEMENT

Adjust as Needed

Audience engagement is a great way to keep track of your time throughout your presentation. Plan all your activities and know when you need to cut back or allow for extra time.

Don't Know? Don't Panic

Inviting questions throughout your presentation can be intimidating, but it allows for a conversation to take place. It opens the space for a two-way dialogue and you'll learn to appreciate knowing what's going through the mind of your audience. Occasionally you'll be asked a question you don't know the answer to. Don't panic. This is a great opportunity to ask the question to the room. This looks gracious because you are trusting that your audience knows the answer. If nobody knows then you can share with them that you haven't been asked that before and would like to follow up with them later.

Always Be You

If you have a natural talent for humor or performance arts, use it to your advantage. Put your stamp on your presentation. Be uniquely you and the audience will love you for it. If you're not a stage artist, don't fear. You can be highly engaging without having to entertain. Don't be afraid to experiment with new ways to involve your audience. They will appreciate your sincerity and interest in involving them.

How can you tell if you've engaged your audience?

- ☐ Complied with your requests
- ☐ Nodded their heads
- ☐ Laughed
- ☐ Engaged when appropriate
- ☐ Multiple voices participated
- ☐ Gave you feedback
- ☐ Approached you after the presentation
- ☐ Fulfilled on your call to action
- ☐ Referred you
- ☐ Connected with you afterwards via phone or email

You're Qualified

Ideally you have someone introduce you as a speaker and that person reads a paragraph you've prepared in advance. This is an endorsement from the introducer and a chance to mention any credentials or credibility statements.

If you don't have the privilege of an introduction it will be fine. Don't worry about making yourself credible. You are at the front of the room and have been vetted in advance. The audience assumes you know your stuff. Feel free to share some of your experience but include it throughout and don't use it as your opening.

PROTIP: Instead of saying, "I'm going to tell you what I've learned," try saying, "I'm going to share with you what I've learned."

05 Reflection

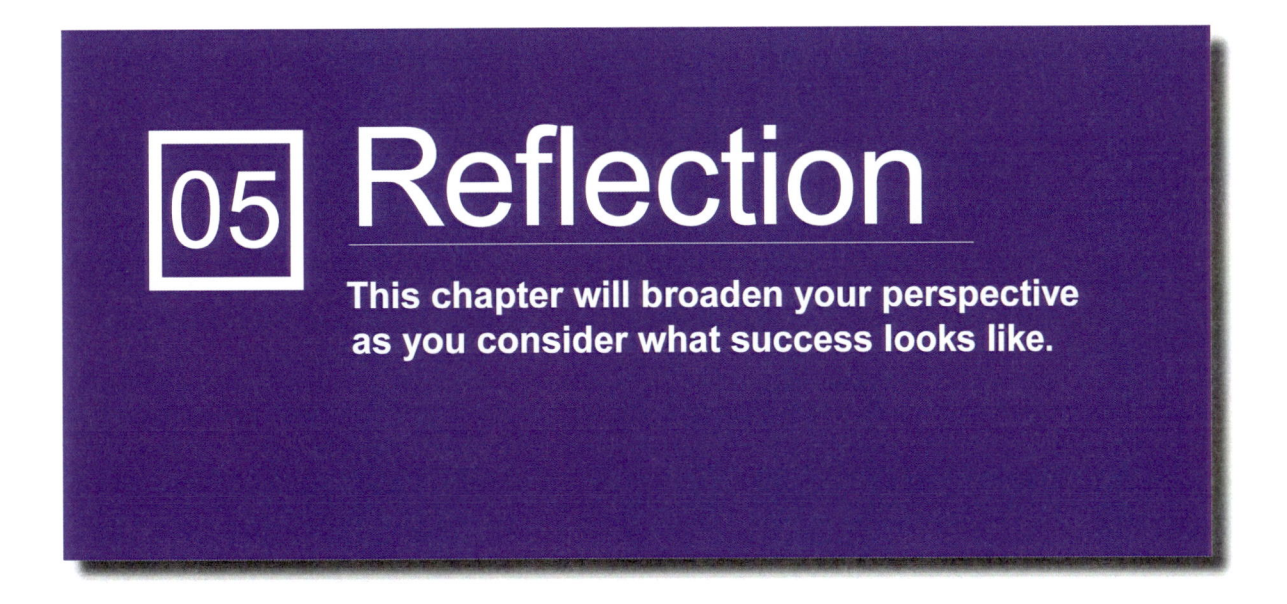

This chapter will broaden your perspective as you consider what success looks like.

"My greatest lessons came to me the hard way. What I thought was failure turned out to be learning I couldn't have paid for."

Sara Krisher

Personal Speaking Assessment

Technical Skills

Date: _____

Rate yourself on each of the below. 1=Needs work   5=Nailed it

Eye Contact Make eye contact with your audience like you would a trusted friend.	1	2	3	4	5
Gestures Freely using your hands to communicate what you are saying.	1	2	3	4	5
Movement Move purposefully with comfort.	1	2	3	4	5
Language Speaking clearly and using words the audience understands.	1	2	3	4	5
Fillers (umm...) Comfortable with pauses and your transitions flow. No nervous fillers.	1	2	3	4	5
Pace Speaking pace is authentic to you. You like to slow down or pause for emphasis.	1	2	3	4	5
Pause Comfortable with silence and you breathe naturally.	1	2	3	4	5
Projection Your volume is audible to the front and back row.	1	2	3	4	5
Tone Using the full range of your voice with variety as you would talking to a friend.	1	2	3	4	5

NOTES

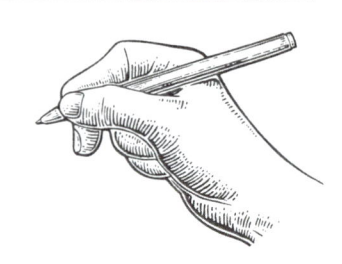

Personal Speaking Assessment
Overall Impression

Rate yourself on each of the below. 1=Needs work   5=Nailed it

Approachability Inviting, friendly, and interested in your audience.	1	2	3	4	5
Confidence Bring your whole self to the front of the room and know your message is of value.	1	2	3	4	5
Authenticity You are the same off stage as you are on stage.	1	2	3	4	5
Credibility You are respected for your experience and know your subject matter.	1	2	3	4	5
Passionate You care about your topic. It's communicated in what you say and how you say it.	1	2	3	4	5
Engagement You find ways to interact with your audience.	1	2	3	4	5
Main Point Your message is understood and the audience walks away knowing what it was all for.	1	2	3	4	5
Timing You know how much time you have to speak and start and end on time.	1	2	3	4	5

NOTES

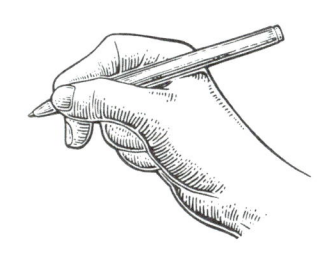

FEEDBACK - WHAT TO ASK FOR

Facts / Observation

Some things I observed about you and your presentation are...

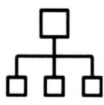

Logical Flow / Organization

One thing I found easy to understand and one thing I found difficult and why

Interpretation / Meaning

As an audience member, I understood your presentation to mean...

Suggestions for Growth

To make your presentation even better, something you might try next time is...

NOTES

How do I know if I hit the target?

Indicators of Success Rate your delivery. 1=needs work 5=Nailed it

I communicated clearly and comfortably	1 2 3 4 5
I handled the unexpected with grace and confidence	1 2 3 4 5
I connected and showed a bit of my personality	1 2 3 4 5
I saw positive body language from the audience	1 2 3 4 5
I felt I was able to build rapport	1 2 3 4 5

Rejection Proof

by Jia Jiang

Dive into this fascinating experiment by author Jia Jiang. His book is a chronicle of his 100 days of rejection and what he learns about overcoming fear.

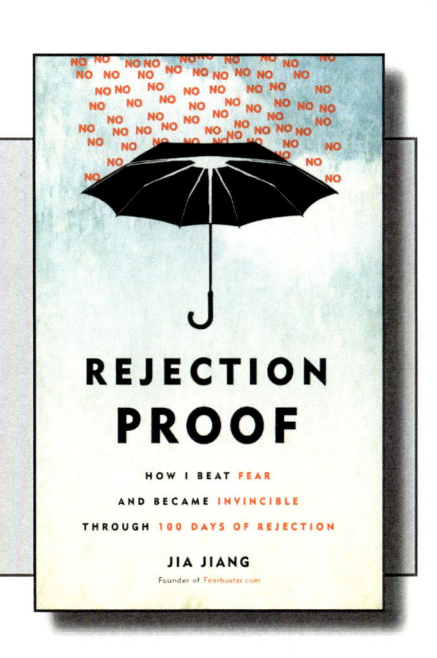

06 Resources

This chapter is a collection of tools, FAQ's and references for your convenience.

"Use your fear. It can take you to the place where you store your courage."

Amelia Earhart

7 C's Worksheet

Critical Point: _____

Captivate	Connect	Consensus	Core
How will you grab their attention?	How can you relate to your audience?	What can you do to bring them with you?	Transition Statement

1

2

What 3 elements support your critical point?

3

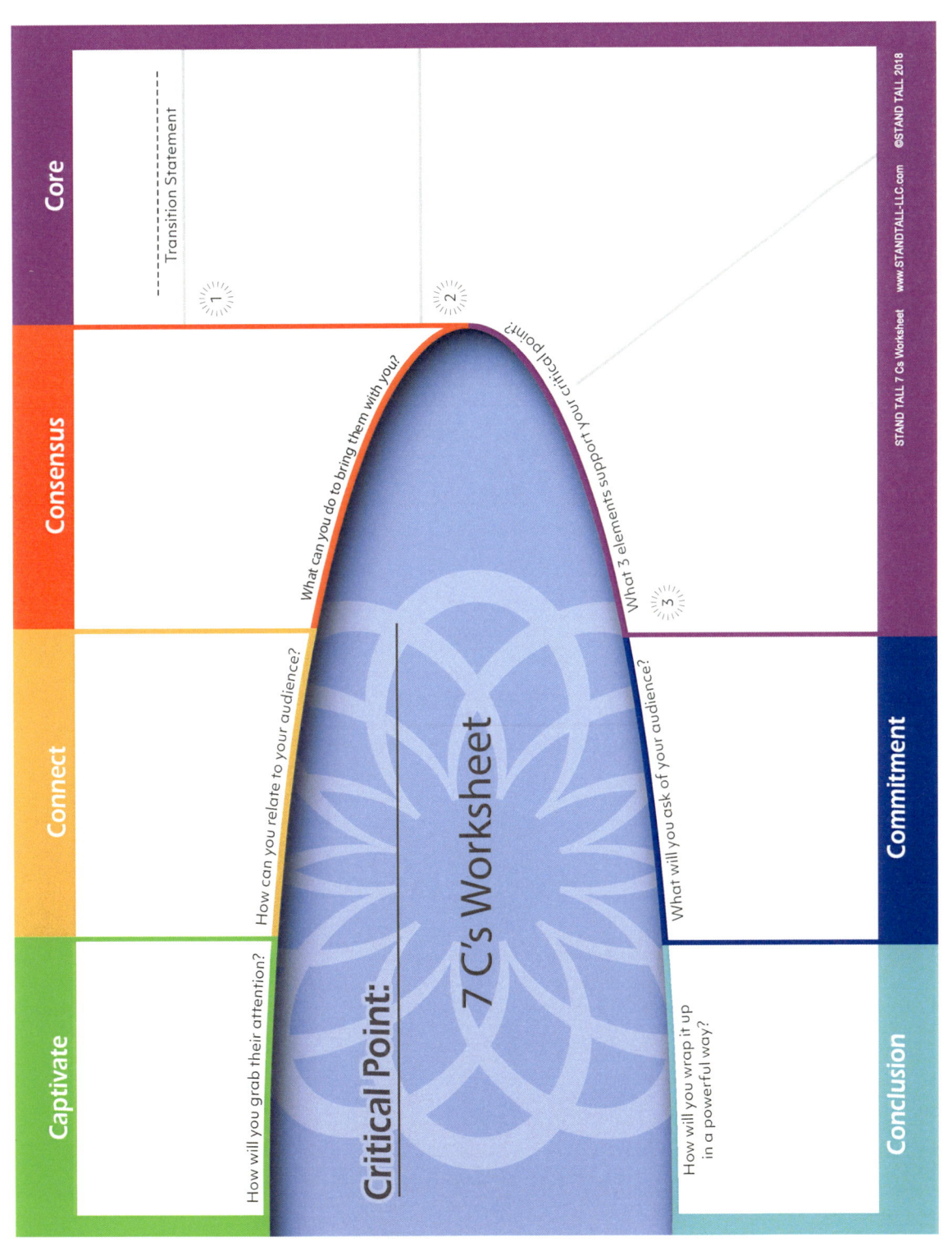

Conclusion	Commitment
How will you wrap it up in a powerful way?	What will you ask of your audience?

STAND TALL 7 Cs Worksheet © STAND TALL 2018 www.STANDTALL-LLC.com

Captivate Your Audience • 75

FAQ's

1. What do I do with my hands?

A great default position for your hands is down at your side. Allow them to rest easy at your side so they aren't locked in front of you when you need to use them.

2. How can I rid myself of using fillers?

Try planning your transitions between points, ideas, or concepts. Knowing how you will move between them can dramatically cut your use of fillers.

3. Are transitions really that important?

Yes, when you thoughtfully plan your transitions you'll naturally have fewer fillers and less anxiety.

4. What happens if I get questions?

It means your audience is engaged and interested in what you have to say.
Decide in advance how you will handle questions and let the audience know.
- You can collect the questions on a whiteboard and answer them at the end.
- You can answer as you go.
- You can ask them to hold their questions until the end.
- You can decide not to take questions.

5. What is a good way to introduce a new point or concept?

Use signal words to make your points easier to follow.
For example; "Next, I'll share with you the top three reasons leaders don't journey to the front of the room. The first reason is…, The second reason is…, Finally, the third reason is…"

6. What's the best way to time my speech?

If it's short you can rehearse the speech and time yourself. If it's long you may want to rehearse and time each part of your speech. This way you know about how long each part takes and can flex if needed in the moment.

7. Can I look at the back wall instead of the people in my audience?

Good eye contact is a nonverbal way to acknowledge your audience. It builds trust when the audience knows you are talking directly to them. Trust is how you make a connection. So the answer is no, try looking your audience in the eyes.

8. Are fillers a big deal?

They can be. Too many fillers like um and ah can distract the audience from hearing your message.

9. Should I apologize upfront for my deficiencies?

Refrain from apologies as it lowers expectations and cues the audience for disappointment before you've even started. Honor your audience by doing your best to communicate your message even if the situation isn't ideal. The ideal speaking situation is the one you have in front of you.

Avoid comments like these because they are a form of apology:
"I didn't get much sleep last night so I'm not sure how this will sound."
"I didn't have the time I would've liked to prepare."
"I forgot my notes so bear with me."

10. What is a pause?

A pause is a mini break (2 - 3 seconds) to breathe or add space between concepts and ideas.

GLOSSARY

Analogy
A comparison between two things, typically for the purpose of explanation or clarification. - "Life is like a box of chocolates." Forrest Gump

Anecdote
A short and amusing or interesting story about a real incident or person with a point.

Anxiety
A feeling of worry, nervousness, or unease, typically about an imminent event or something with an uncertain outcome.

Audience centric
The audience is the center of the speech and the content is highly relevant to them.

Audience Connection
Building rapport, being relatable with stories, visuals, activities, etc.

Audience Engagement
The extent to which audience members are interested or actively involved in your message.

Authenticity
Being 'you' on or off stage.

Confidence
Authentic expression.

Content Development
The process of researching, writing, gathering, organizing, and editing information for your speech.

Courage
Mental or moral strength to venture, persevere, and withstand danger, fear, or difficulty.

Enjoyment
The state or process of taking pleasure in something.

Experience
Skill or knowledge that you get by doing something.

Explicit Knowledge
Knowledge that is easy to communicate, store, and distribute and is the knowledge found in books, on the web, and other visual and oral means.

Glossophobia
Fear of public speaking.

Integrity
The quality or state of being complete or undivided. (Your words are in alignment with your tone and body language.)

Lectern
A tall stand with a sloping top to hold a book or notes, and from which someone, typically a preacher or lecturer, can read while standing up.

Metaphor
A figure of speech that describes an object or action in a way that isn't literally true, but helps explain an idea or make a comparison.

Narrative
A spoken or written account of connected events; a story.

Perfection
The state of being complete and correct in every way.

Podium
A small platform on which a person may stand to be seen by an audience, as when making a speech or conducting an orchestra.

Preparation
The action or process of making ready or being made ready for use or consideration.

Purpose
The reason for which something is done or created or for which something exists.

Risk
An uncertain event or condition that, if it occurs, has an effect on at least one objective.

Segue
To make a transition without interruption from one activity, topic, scene, or part to another.

Self-efficacy
One's belief in one's ability to succeed in specific situations or accomplish a task.

Self-assessment
Assessment or evaluation of oneself or one's actions and attitudes, in particular, of one's performance at a job or learning task considered in relation to an objective standard.

Self-compassion
Self-compassion is extending compassion to one's self in instances of perceived inadequacy, failure, or general suffering.

Self-doubt
Lack of confidence in oneself and one's abilities.

Simile
A common figure of speech that explicitly compares two things usually considered different. Most similes are introduced by like or as: "The realization hit me like a bucket of cold water."

Tacit Knowledge
All of the collective know-how, techniques, processes and difficult to articulate expertise that is part of an individual's knowledge base.

Technical Skills
The ability to carry out the task associated with technical aspects for a role such as speaking.

Transition
The process or a period of changing from one state or condition to another.

Trust
Firm belief in the reliability, truth, ability, or strength of someone or something.

Vulnerability
The quality or state of being exposed to the possibility of being attacked or harmed, either physically or emotionally.

REFERENCES

Books

15	*The Confidence Gap* by Russ Harris
41	*Taming your Gremlin* by Rick Carson
73	*Rejection Proof* by Jia Jiang

Pro Tips

15	Your audience wants you to succeed
36	To avoid perfection, don't over craft your written words and spend too much time with them.
44	Smile because it puts others at ease and it's a non-verbal invitation for your audience to approach you.
64	Memorize your opening sentences to get you started smoothly.
68	Instead of saying, "I'm going to tell you what I've learned," try saying, "I'm going to share with you what I've learned."

Quotes

13	"No matter what people tell you, words and ideas can change the world." Robin Williams
14	"Feel the fear and do it anyway." Susan Jeffers
16	"A person often meets his destiny on the road he took to avoid it." Jean de La Fontaine
17	"Everything you want is on the other side of fear." Jack Canfield
23	"Tacit knowledge is like teaching someone to ride a bike. It requires more than the written word." Sara Krisher
24	"Courage is contagious. Every time we choose courage, we make everyone around us a little better and the world a little braver." Brene Brown
25	"Uncertainty is the root of all progress and all growth. As the old adage goes, the man who believes he knows everything learns nothing. We cannot learn anything without first not knowing something." Mark Manson

REFERENCES CONTINUED

Quotes

31	"When seen through a wider lens, creativity is not simply 'the arts', it is a natural state and condition that arises in all human beings when their level of fear is diminshed." Peter Himmelman
33	"No matter how much you yearn to do everything flawlessly, the stage will teach you humility." Sara Krisher
41	"If you are always trying to be normal you will never know how amazing you can be." Maya Angelou
53	"Normal and average are plain and boring. Special and different is exciting and sets you apart." Danika Socwell
60	"Every story needs a point and every point needs a story." Unknown
69	"My greatest lessons came to me the hard way. What I thought was failure turned out to be learning I couldn't have paid for."Sara Krisher
74	"Use your fear. It can take you to the place where you store your courage." Amelia Earhart

Ted Talks

24	The Power of Vulnerability https://www.ted.com/talks/brene_brown_on_vulnerability
27	Power Pose for more Confidence https://www.ted.com/talks/amy_cuddy_your_body_language_shapes_who_you_are
62	The Art of Speaking https://www.youtube.com/watch?v=8S0FDjFBj8o&vl=en